Energy
Reactions
in the Kitchen

Ann McCallum Staats, M.Ed.

Consultants

Benjamin Andrews
Geologist and Associate Curator of Rocks and Ores
National Museum of Natural History

Cheryl Lane, M.Ed.
Seventh Grade Science Teacher
Chino Valley Unified School District

Michelle Wertman, M.S.Ed.
Literacy Specialist
New York City Public Schools

Publishing Credits

Rachelle Cracchiolo, M.S.Ed., *Publisher*
Emily R. Smith, M.A.Ed., *SVP of Content Development*
Véronique Bos, *VP of Creative*
Dani Neiley, *Editor*
Robin Erickson, *Senior Art Director*
Jill Malcolm, *Senior Graphic Designer*

Smithsonian Enterprises

Avery Naughton, Licensing Coordinator
Paige Towler, Editorial Lead
Jill Corcoran, Senior Director, Licensed Publishing
Brigid Ferraro, Vice President of New Business and Licensing
Carol LeBlanc, President

Image Credits: all images from Shutterstock and/or iStock

Library of Congress Control Number available upon request.

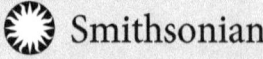

5482 Argosy Avenue
Huntington Beach, CA 92649
www.tcmpub.com
ISBN 979-8-7659-6877-2
© 2025 Teacher Created Materials, Inc.

Table of Contents

Setting the Table

No matter where people live, how they live, or who they live with, they all share one thing in common: they eat food. People combine various ingredients to create the best-tasting food. But what *is* food? How do simple ingredients undergo complex changes in the kitchen?

On a chemical level, food is made up of atoms and molecules. These atoms and molecules combine into various chemicals that interact with one another. They might be naturally occurring chemicals, such as proteins, carbohydrates, or fats. These are **macronutrients**. Or they might be **micronutrients**, such as vitamins and minerals. Food can also contain other ingredients that might be human-made. (This is true for soda and pepperoni, which we'll get into later!)

Methods of food preparation involve two kinds of reactions that use energy. First, physical reactions in the kitchen can change how food looks without changing the molecules. This is true for foods like ice cream and butter. Second, chemical reactions cause permanent changes to molecules. Transforming a batter into a cake or grilling a steak are two examples of chemical changes. Let's dig into some ingredients and dishes that undergo these reactions!

SCIENCE

Tasty

Think of all the different flavors you enjoy. You can taste them thanks to the tiny bumps on your tongue called *papillae*, where taste buds are found. On average, humans have 2,000 to 10,000 taste buds. Children have more taste buds when they are younger. The number decreases as a person ages.

taste buds

Ways of Preparing Food

Many methods exist for preparing food. And when food is cooked, it undergoes changes that involve chemical reactions. For example, you might fry onion rings, bake cookies, or boil oatmeal. In each of these cases, cooking the food involves an **endothermic reaction**. In this type of reaction, heat is a key factor. The food absorbs heat, causing a permanent chemical change. To cook certain types of food, different heating methods are used.

Flour-based foods usually need an even heat source. That is why cookies, pies, bread, and cakes are baked in an oven where they can be surrounded by heat. During this cooking process, the outer surface of a dough or batter bakes faster than the middle. So, while the outside may look done, the inside may still be undercooked. To check that the inside is cooked, bakers often insert a toothpick into the middle.

oven

Frying and grilling are other methods of cooking. A fat, such as butter or vegetable oil, is often needed for frying. This creates a barrier that prevents food from sticking to hot pans. Some special equipment, such as nonstick frying pans, have coatings on them that allow food to be heated without sticking. When using a grill, direct and intense heat is applied to food for a short time. Meats and vegetables are often cooked on grills.

Deep-frying involves covering food in hot oil to cook it.

Gas grills use flames to cook food.

Unique Methods

Baking, frying, grilling, and microwaving are not the only ways to prepare food. Here are a few unique food and drink preparation methods.

Zing! Some foods like sauerkraut and kimchi are prepared through fermentation. Fermentation uses bacteria to change the sugars and starches in food to lactic acid. Lactic acid is what gives these foods their tangy, sour taste. To make sauerkraut, cabbage is finely shredded and combined with salt. Kimchi is made the same way, but other vegetables and spices are added. Then, the mixture is put into an airtight jar. Over time, the salty brine allows the bacteria to get to work. The bacteria creates acid and releases carbon dioxide as it changes the food. The carbon dioxide builds up pressure, so the jar will need to be opened occasionally to release it. Fermentation can take anywhere from 3–6 weeks.

kimchi

sauerkraut

Fizz! The sharp, bubbly effect in sodas comes from carbon dioxide gas. At a soda factory, the gas is forced into each beverage using pressure and cool temperatures. When the gas is trapped inside a bottle or can, it can't escape. But when the container is opened and exposed to the air, you'll hear the bubbles inside fizzing.

Spicy! Pepperoni is a blend of meat that is cured rather than cooked. When beef, pork, or other meat is ground up, lactic acid is mixed in. This makes the meat more acidic and helps **preserve** it. Salt is added too, removing water and slowing down harmful bacteria growth. The meat is then put into **casings**, where it gets air-dried and then smoked for a unique flavor.

When pepperoni is put into casings, it is hung to air-dry for a few days to a few weeks.

All About Fruits and Vegetables

It's Taco Tuesday, and you want some guacamole to put on your tacos. You remember that there is some in the fridge from yesterday. But when you open it, you see that it has changed colors!

Many fruits and vegetables turn brown when they are cut, heated, or cooled. (Or, in the case of the avocado in the guacamole, as they get older.) This can also happen if you slice an apple or let a banana sit on the counter for too long. This browning is a chemical reaction known as enzymatic browning. This is due to certain molecules called **enzymes**. When a certain enzyme found in fruits and vegetables comes into contact with oxygen, it causes a chemical reaction. A substance called *melanin* is produced, creating the brown color in fruits and vegetables. Melanin is the same substance that is responsible for brown hair, eyes, and skin.

Guacamole changes from bright green to brown over time.

If cut apple slices are left out long enough, the tops and sides will begin to turn brown.

There are ways to stop or slow down this browning reaction. Lowering the temperature of a fridge can decrease the browning enzyme activity in some foods. These enzymes need water to work properly, so drying fruits and vegetables can help. Packaging that prevents oxygen from getting in reduces the amount of browning. Finally, adding an acid like lemon juice or vinegar can interfere with the enzyme and stop the reaction from happening.

How can lemon juice or vinegar stop browning? The answer lies in acidity. The **pH scale**, which goes from 0 to 14, determines how acidic or **alkaline** a substance is. For reference, pure water measures right in the middle at 7.0. It is neutral because it is neither acidic nor alkaline. Most foods are mildly acidic with pH values slightly less than 7.

Lemon juice, on the other hand, has a pH of around 2 to 3. Lemons are strongly acidic. That is why they have a sour taste that might make you pucker your lips! Acids can be powerful, and that's exactly why lemon juice works to stop fruit from browning. Other foods, including vinegar, limes, and grapefruit, are acidic as well. Highly acidic foods tend to taste sour or tangy.

Acids can create other unique reactions. One example occurs when citrus juice is used on seafood. Chunks of raw shrimp or fish can be marinated in lemon or lime juice until they turn **opaque**. The low pH of the citrus juice changes the structure of the protein. It becomes "cooked" without heat. The acid changes the texture of the marinated seafood, making it similar to the texture of grilled or cooked seafood.

The pH Scale

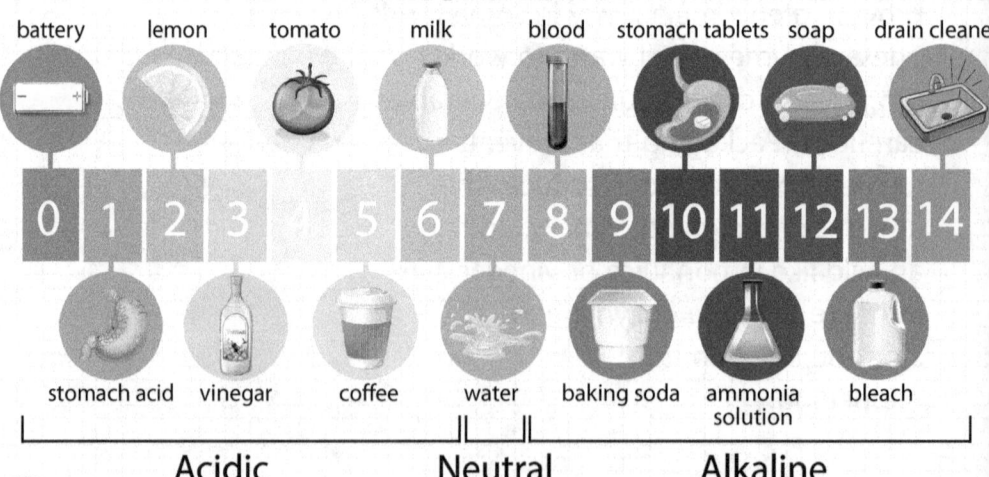

battery   lemon   tomato   milk   blood   stomach tablets   soap   drain cleaner

0 1 2 3 5 6 7 8 9 10 11 12 13 14

stomach acid   vinegar   coffee   water   baking soda   ammonia solution   bleach

Acidic   Neutral   Alkaline

Ceviche recipes combine fish cooked in citrus juice with tomatoes, onions, cilantro, avocado, jalapeño, and cucumber.

FUN FACT

A chemical reaction occurs when you combine acidic and basic substances. Have you ever heard of combining baking soda with vinegar? This mixture can create a minor explosion. That's because baking soda is alkaline and vinegar is acidic, so mixing the two releases carbon dioxide bubbles.

Protein Power

Crack! Sizzle! From frying an egg to grilling a hamburger, proteins undergo massive transformations in the kitchen. Chicken, beef, pork, fish, and turkey are common protein choices. Let's take a look at what makes up these proteins and how they can change.

Meats are made of molecules called *amino acids* that link up into chains of protein. Amino acids are necessary sources of energy for human bodies. For instance, bodies can build and repair muscles and bones thanks to amino acids. While our bodies can make hundreds of amino acids, we cannot make essential amino acids. These essential nutrients must come from the food we eat. Meat and fish are both good sources of essential amino acids.

Meats and eggs are common sources of protein, but other options include nuts, beans, and peas.

Steak can be cooked to different levels.

rare   medium-rare   medium   medium-well   well done

When meats are roasted, fried, or grilled, the protein molecules begin to vibrate faster in the heat. This triggers a chemical reaction, forcing the protein's building blocks to rearrange. Some of the less stable bonds between the molecules break. The tight, folded chains begin to unwind. This process of altering the shape of a protein is called *denaturation*. As this process occurs, the meat cooks, and the flavor and smell of the meat changes. Plus, as the meat cooks, heat kills any harmful bacteria in it. Food safety experts recommend cooking different protein sources to different internal temperatures. For example, steak is safe to eat when it reaches 62.8 °C (145 °F).

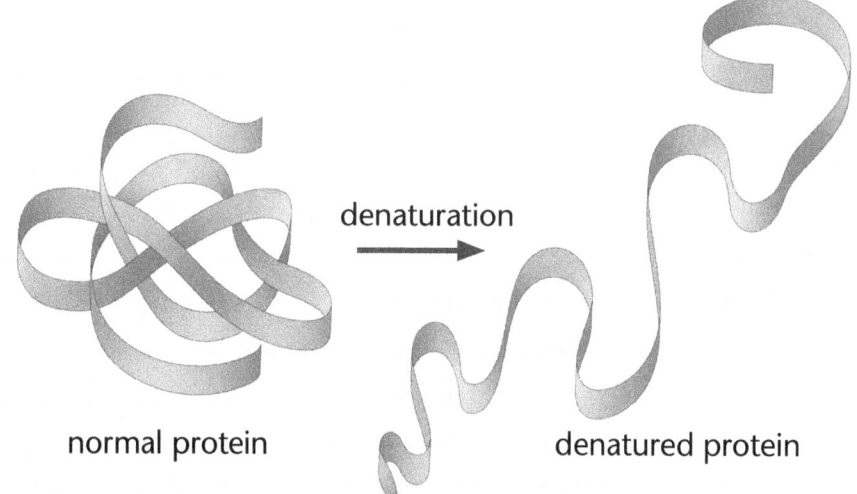

denaturation

normal protein   denatured protein

The Maillard Reaction

It's lunchtime, so you take a plate full of hamburger patties out of the fridge. Your first step is to heat a frying pan on the stove with some oil. When the surface is piping hot, you place the burgers in the pan, and the meat sizzles. When you flip the burgers, you see a brown crust on the outside of each patty. The food smells amazing, and your stomach growls.

A chemical reaction causes food to become brown, **aromatic**, and delicious. It's called the *Maillard reaction*, and it is also known as the browning reaction. This reaction occurs when heat interacts with amino acids and simple sugars found in protein. Meats are not the only type of food that undergoes this reaction. This reaction occurs in bread, roasted vegetables, cookies, and even coffee.

Here's a closer look at what happens when a hamburger patty experiences this reaction. The heat from the pan sets off a series of chemical reactions. New and unstable molecules form, which soon break down and create different molecules. This is what creates a brown crust on the surface of the meat. Then, the meat turns from red to pink inside. If the meat is cooked even longer, the inside will change from pink to brown or gray. In the end, this process changes both color and taste, creating a more flavorful protein.

Vegetables turn brown and crispy when roasted in an oven.

The tops of these scallops were seared in a hot pan and turned brown.

Food Engineering

There are many types of engineering jobs—and one even exists for food! Food engineers have a wide range of jobs. They might figure out the **logistics** of producing and handling food. They might design a system of transportation for food so that it can be delivered fresh and undamaged. They might also work on food packaging.

Some food engineers work in factories.

Baked Goods

Baking a cake, cookies, or bread is a delicious—and exact—science experiment. If too much or too little of an ingredient is added, you may not get the results you were hoping for. During the cooking process, batter or dough undergoes a chemical reaction to form something entirely new.

This process may start with mixing a fat, such as butter, with sugar. Next, stirring in eggs holds everything together. The stirring motion adds air to the batter or dough. Adding flour provides structure. **Leavening agents**, such as baking powder and baking soda, release carbon dioxide bubbles that help make the batter or dough light and fluffy. They also help it expand. Pouring the mixture into a baking pan and putting it in the oven is the last step. With even heat, the mixture rises, sets firmly into shape, and browns on the outside.

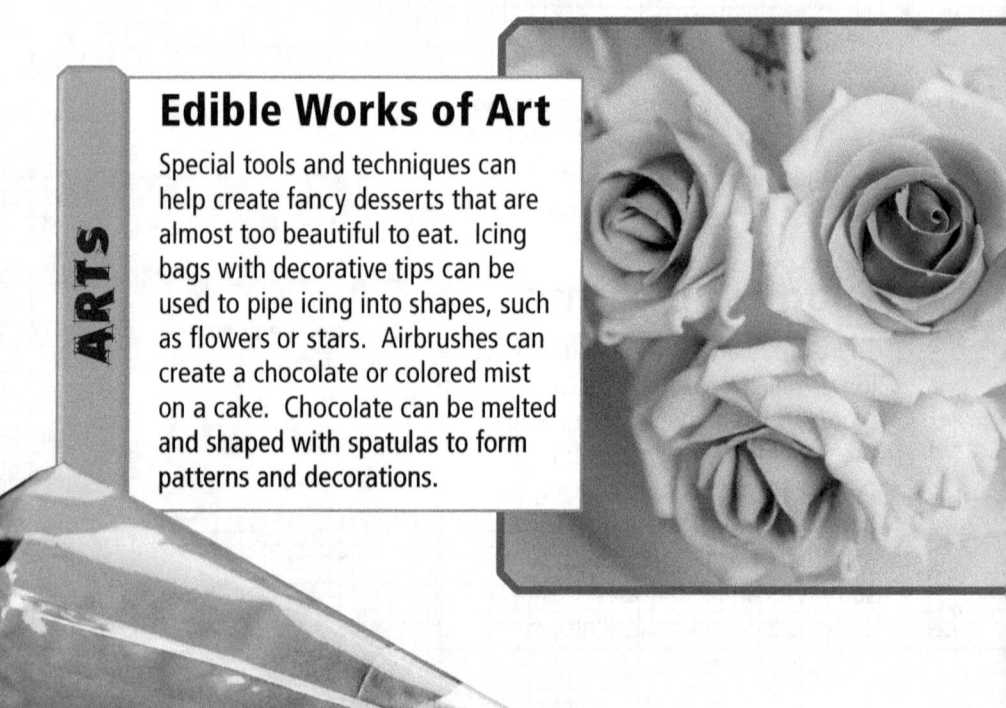

ARTS

Edible Works of Art

Special tools and techniques can help create fancy desserts that are almost too beautiful to eat. Icing bags with decorative tips can be used to pipe icing into shapes, such as flowers or stars. Airbrushes can create a chocolate or colored mist on a cake. Chocolate can be melted and shaped with spatulas to form patterns and decorations.

If doughs and batters are mixed too much, the air will be taken out and they will become dense and tough.

Introducing Gluten

Flour is made from grains, nuts, or beans. Wheat flour, the most common type, contains mostly starch and proteins. When wheat flour is mixed with water, proteins in the flour form a new protein called *gluten*. The molecules in gluten develop long chains and a webbed structure that holds baked goods together. The creation of gluten is what makes the dough or batter stretchy. This quality helps trap air or carbon dioxide bubbles that come from mixing or using leavening agents.

Pizza dough is stretched to make gluten form, allowing the dough to be easily rolled out.

Getting a Rise out of It

How does a gooey batter turn into a fluffy cake? This rise is all thanks to leavening agents. These substances are added to a batter before the baking stage. They help the batter expand by releasing gas when they are mixed with liquid, acid, or heat.

One leavening agent is yeast, which is popular for making bread. Yeast is made of tiny one-cell organisms. It needs food, moisture, and warmth to grow. It also needs time, which bakers call *proofing*. When yeast consumes food, especially sugar, it produces carbon dioxide gas and ethanol. This process is called *fermentation*, and it traps gas bubbles inside the dough. When dough is put in the oven to bake, the yeast dies off but leaves the bread light and airy.

types of yeast

Egyptian sun bread is traditionally left outside to rise in the sun.

Baking soda is another leavening agent. It needs to be mixed with an acid to produce gas. That's why you might find lemon juice or buttermilk in certain recipes. These acids are added to the batter to help baking soda make carbon dioxide bubbles.

baking soda

Baking powder can also be used to help dough or batter rise. Baking powder comes with a dry acid already added to it. So, there is no need to add an acid like you would with baking soda.

baking powder

The advantage of baking powder and baking soda is that they work much faster than yeast. Some recipes may call for both ingredients to maximize the rise of a baked good.

Cake batter rises in the heat of an oven.

Milking It

Dairy products include milk, butter, and cheese. These foods are often **savory** and can be used in various recipes or consumed on their own. Milk is the key to creating butter and cheese through chemical reactions.

In the United States, most milk is produced by cows. Milk is about 88 percent water. The remainder includes high-fat cream, proteins, **lactose**, vitamins, and minerals. All milk is an emulsion, meaning it is a mixture of a liquid within a liquid. Tiny droplets of fat called *globules* are suspended throughout the milk.

Before milk is bottled and shipped to stores, it is pasteurized. It is heated briefly to kill dangerous bacteria and then cooled quickly. The makeup of the milk doesn't change during this process, so it is not considered a chemical reaction.

pasteurization equipment

Milk Percentages

What is the difference between whole, two percent, one percent, and skim milk? The taste, thickness, and amount of **calories** all differ. For starters, whole milk is the closest match to milk straight from a cow. It is made of about 3.5 percent milk fat and will have the most calories. As you go from two percent to skim milk, fat gets taken out, and calories are reduced.

When Things Go Bad

Pasteurizing milk kills off most of the bacteria, but it doesn't get rid of it entirely. Some harmless bacteria remain. Over time, this bacteria multiplies. It feeds off the lactose in milk, making the milk more acidic. The pH decreases and causes the milk proteins to change structure. This is a chemical change because the protein **coagulates**. Solid, lumpy bits called *curds* form. When milk fully spoils, it turns into white curds and a watery, yellowish **whey**. Plus, it tastes and smells sour.

curds and whey

Cheese, Please!

All cheeses start as milk. Helpful bacteria are added to make the milk break down, and a chemical reaction separates it into curds and whey. This might sound a lot like spoiled milk, but the mixture does not have harmful bacteria in it. The curds are taken out of the whey and gently cooked, and salt is added to preserve them. This is how soft cheeses, such as cream cheese and cottage cheese, are made. For hard cheeses, the curds are put into molds and stored in a cool place to age, dry out, and develop flavor. This is how firm cheeses, such as sharp cheddar or Parmesan, are made.

storing cheeses for aging

Cheeses come in many shapes, colors, and flavors!

Creamy Ice Cream

Making ice cream is a physical change. Milk and cream transform from a liquid to a smooth solid without becoming too hard. First, large machines **homogenize** the liquid to create even fat droplets. This prevents clumps of fat from forming. Next, high-speed blades spin to prevent ice crystals from forming and add air to the mix.

finished ice cream coming out of a machine

Better with Butter

The cream in fresh milk is used to make solid butter. The cream gets **skimmed** off, put into a container, and **churned**. During this process, globules of fat start to bump into one another. With time and force, the fat begins to clump together. Soon, solid butter forms alongside leftover buttermilk, a watery substance with very little fat. The solid butter is pressed to remove moisture and put into molds.

Making butter is a physical change rather than a chemical change. Cream changes from a liquid to a solid without changing its chemical makeup. Plus, it can easily be reversed. Think of how easy it is to melt butter. And if you take melted butter and mix it with buttermilk for long enough, you'll end up with cream again!

Time to Eat!

The chopping, mixing, and cooking is done. The food's ready, and it's time to eat! Physical and chemical changes in the food have produced delicious smells and mouthwatering tastes. Every bite includes macronutrients and micronutrients. These nutrients keep our bodies healthy and provide energy.

When you're hungry, it's hard to think about the complex science behind a plate full of food. But food is made up of matter. Each atom and molecule in an ingredient behaves and reacts in a series of actions. And the result is the finished food we eat. Sometimes, heat makes molecules vibrate faster, causing permanent or reversible changes. Fried eggs, baked goods, and grilled meats all experience permanent chemical changes. Chocolate and butter can experience reversible physical changes. Other times, cooling or freezing food leads to a physical change. This is how ice cream turns into a solid from a liquid. Ingredients can also be added to food to trigger a reaction. Something acidic, such as lemon juice, can be added to cake batter to help it rise or to "cook" raw fish.

Before biting into your next meal, think about the ingredients inside. What reactions occurred to make the food you're going to eat? Chances are that a physical or chemical reaction happened!

STEAM CHALLENGE

Define the Problem

Restaurant workers are looking to learn more about the acidity and alkalinity of common cleaning substances, including baking soda, dish soap, hydrogen peroxide, vinegar, and more. They want to create a new combination of substances that results in a chemical change. Your job is to test six materials for their acidity or alkalinity. Then, you will create a combination of the materials and evaluate it for chemical changes.

Constraints: You may only use the materials that are provided to you.

Criteria: You must test the materials to determine whether they are basic, acidic, or neutral. Then, you will create a combination of the materials. Your resulting combination must have a visible chemical change.

Research and Brainstorm

What are acids and bases, and how do their ions interact with one another? What is a pH scale? What is a chemical change, and how can you create one?

Design and Build

Work with a partner to predict the acidity and alkalinity of the available materials and write your predictions. Together, determine which materials you plan to combine to monitor for chemical changes. Write these materials, and then collect them to prepare for a test.

Test and Improve

Using litmus paper, test your materials. Are they basic, acidic, or neutral? Combine your selected materials, check for a chemical change, and record your results. Did it result in a chemical change? What is the pH of the solution? What changes can you make? Adjust the materials, and retest as needed.

Reflect and Share

Which items resulted in a chemical change? Why do you think that happened? What part of this challenge did you find most interesting? What was challenging? How did you and your partner's ideas complement each other?

Glossary

alkaline—of, relating to, or having the characteristics of a basic substance with a pH of more than 7

aromatic—having a pleasant and distinctive smell

calories—units of energy, often used to express the nutritional value of food

casings—materials that cover the fillings of sausages or cured meats

churned—rapidly mixed or turned

coagulates—changes into a solid or partly solid state

endothermic reaction—a chemical reaction in which reactants absorb heat and form new products

enzymes—substances, such as proteins, that help speed up chemical reactions

homogenize—to break up the fat of milk into particles

lactose—a type of sugar that is present in milk

leavening agents—substances that cause doughs and batters to expand by releasing gas

logistics—the coordination of something involving many people, facilities, or supplies

macronutrients—the fats, proteins, and carbohydrates human bodies need for energy in large amounts

micronutrients—chemical elements, such as vitamins and minerals, found in food that are essential for human bodies in small amounts

opaque—not transparent; not letting light through

pH scale—a system of measurement that determines how acidic or basic a substance is

preserve—to prepare something in such a way that it can be kept for future use

savory—pleasing to the taste or smell; tasting salty or spicy rather than sweet

skimmed—removed something from the surface of a liquid

whey—the watery part of milk that separates after the milk has formed curds, especially in the process of making cheese

Index

CAREER ADVICE
from Smithsonian

Do you want to conduct experiments and be a scientist?

Here are some tips to keep in mind for the future.

"Experiments can be messy! But that makes them fun and helps us learn about nature. Sometimes, the ideas that are the most exciting take a lot of work. Push yourself in classes and keep trying."

– Benjamin Andrews, Geologist, National Museum of Natural History

"Pay attention to how your actions affect or change the world around you."

– Cari Corrigan, Geologist, National Museum of Natural History